Soccer
in
North
America

By
Mike Kennedy
with Mark Stewart

NORWOODHOUSE PRESS

Norwood House Press, P.O. Box 316598, Chicago, Illinois 60631

For information regarding Norwood House Press,
please visit our website at: www.norwoodhousepress.com or call 866-565-2900.

Photo Credits:
  All interior photos provided by Getty Images.
Cover Photos:
  Top Left: Merlin/Topps Europe Ltd.
  Top Right: Washington Post/Getty Images.
  Bottom Left: El Universal via Getty Images.
  Bottom Right: The Upper Deck Company.
The soccer memorabilia photographed for this book is part of the authors' collections:
  Page 10) Marquez: Topps Trading Cards.
  Page 12) Sanchez: The Upper Deck Company; Hamm: Soccer Jr. Magazine;
                Lilly: Sports Illustrated for Kids/TIME Inc.; Sanon: Panini.
  Page 13) Lalas: The Upper Deck Company; De Rosario: The Upper Deck Company;
                Donovan: Topps Trading Cards; Joseph: The Upper Deck Company.

Designer: Ron Jaffe
Project Management: Black Book Partners, LLC
Editorial Production: Jessica McCulloch
Special thanks to Ben and Bill Gould

Library of Congress Cataloging-in-Publication Data
    Kennedy, Mike, 1965-
    Soccer in North America / by Mike Kennedy with Mark Stewart.
        p. cm. -- (Smart about sports)
    Includes bibliographical references and index.
    Summary: "An introductory look at the soccer teams, and their fans, of
    countries in North America. Includes a brief history, facts, photos,
    records, and glossary"--Provided by publisher.
     ISBN-13: 978-1-59953-444-2 (library edition : alk. paper)
     ISBN-10: 1-59953-444-4 (library edition : alk. paper)
     1. Soccer--United States--History. 2. Soccer--History. I. Stewart, Mark,
    1960- II. Title.
     GV944.U5K38 2011
     796.334097--dc22

                                        2010045827

Manufactured in the United States of America in North Mankato, Minnesota.
170N–012011

Contents

Words in **bold type** are defined on page 24.

Soccer has become very popular in the United States.

Where in the World?

People in North America enjoy many sports. But no sport is growing faster than soccer. Millions of boys and girls love to play soccer. They follow soccer around the world, too.

Once Upon a Time

Soccer came to North America in the 1800s. People from Europe traveled across the Atlantic Ocean to find a new life. Playing soccer reminded them of home. Anyone could play. All they needed was a ball!

The United States soccer team takes the field before a 1934 game.

Fans watch a game at Azteca Stadium.

At the Stadium

Azteca Stadium in Mexico is one of the biggest stadiums in the world. It holds more than 100,000 people. The stadium was home to the **World Cup** in 1970 and 1986.

Town & Country

RAFAEL **MARQUEZ**

77 DEFENCE   **22** ATTACK

Like many soccer stars, Rafael Marquez plays for two teams at the same time. When his home country of Mexico has a match, he joins the **national team**. In 2010, he also played for a **club** in the United States.

Rafael Marquez plays for his team in the United States.

Shoe Box

The soccer collection on these pages belongs to the authors. It shows some of the top North American stars.

Hugo Sanchez

Striker • Mexico
Hugo Sanchez scored 427 goals. Fans called him "Hu-GOL."

Mia Hamm

Striker
• United States
Many believe Mia Hamm was the best female player in soccer history.

Kristine Lilly

Midfielder
• United States
No one played more games for Team USA than Kristine Lilly.

Emmanuel Sanon

Striker • Haiti
"Manno" Sanon was Haiti's most exciting goal scorer.

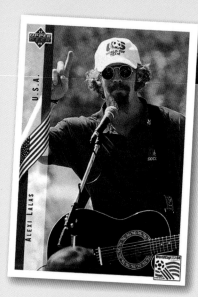

Alexei Lalas

Defender • United States
Soccer fans loved
Alexei Lalas for his
hard play and his
wild hairstyle.

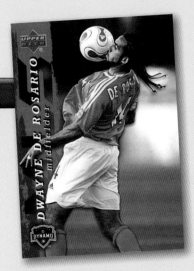

Dwayne De Rosario

Midfielder • Canada
Dwayne De Rosario
became famous for his
game-winning goals.

Landon Donovan

Midfielder
• United States
Landon Donovan
was a hero to soccer
fans across the
United States.

Shalrie Joseph

Midfielder • Grenada
Shalrie Joseph's smart
defense made him
a great leader.

Can't Touch This

The job of a goalkeeper is to keep the other team from scoring goals. Only goalkeepers are allowed to use their hands to make "saves." Teammates can make saves, too. But they may not use their arms or hands.

Marius Fausta of Guadeloupe makes a save.

15

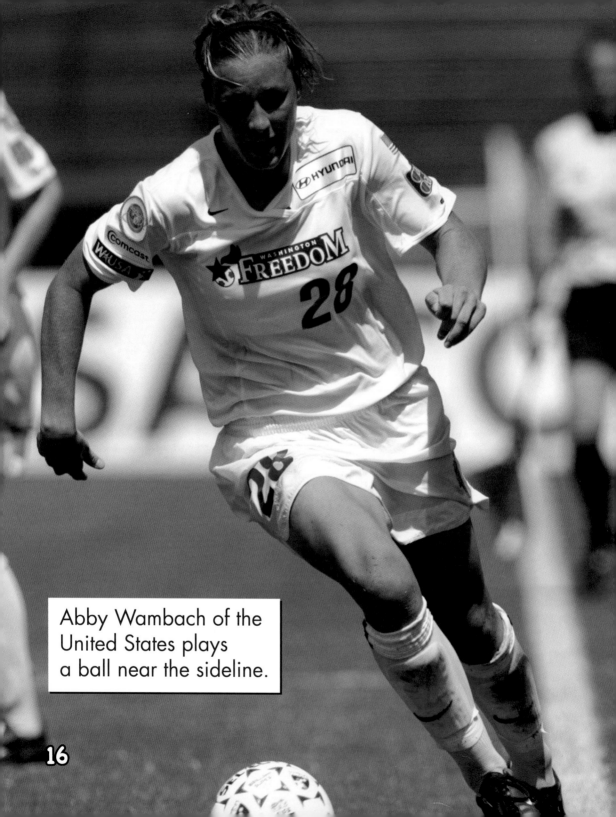

Abby Wambach of the United States plays a ball near the sideline.

Just For Kicks

Watching soccer is more fun when you know some of the rules:

- A ball is out of bounds when it rolls over the **sideline**.

- Another name for the sideline is the "Touchline."

- The ball must be all the way over the line for play to stop.

- A player can be out of bounds as long as the ball is not.

On the Map

Girls and boys play soccer all over North America, including these places:

 Canada

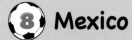 Jamaica

2 Cuba

8 Mexico

3 Dominican Republic

9 Puerto Rico

4 Grenada

10 Trinidad and Tobago

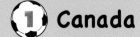 Guadeloupe

11 United States

6 Haiti

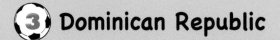

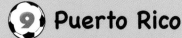

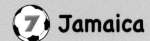

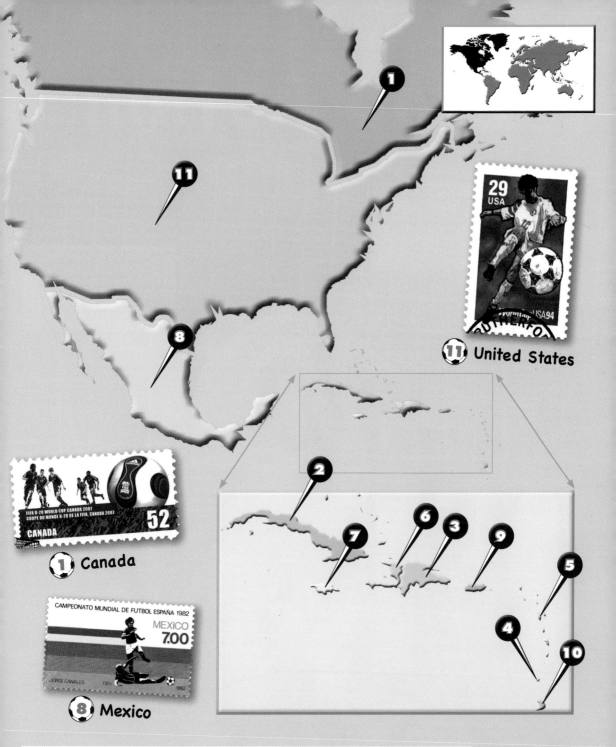

11 United States

1 Canada

8 Mexico

Many countries have their own soccer stamps!

Stop Action

Landon Donovan of the United States scores a goal.

Soccer shoes have studs on the bottom.

We Won!

North America has some of the best teams in the world!

Men's Soccer	CONCACAF* Champion	Olympic** Champion
Mexico	1965, 1971, 1977, 1993, 1996, 1998, 2003, & 2009	
Haiti	1973	
Canada	1985 & 2000	1904
United States	1991, 2002, 2005 & 2007	

Women's Soccer	World Cup Champion	Olympic Champion
United States	1991 & 1999	1996, 2004, & 2008

* CONCACAF stands for Confederation of North, Central American, and Caribbean Association Football. It is made up of national teams from these regions.

** The Olympics are a worldwide sports competition. Soccer has been part of the Olympics since 1900.

Team USA celebrates a win.

23

Soccer Words

CLUB
Another word for team.

NATIONAL TEAM
A team made up of players from the same country.

SIDELINE
The lines that run the length of each side of a soccer field.

WORLD CUP
The tournament that decides the world champion of soccer. The World Cup is played every four years.

Index

Photos are on **bold** numbered pages.

Learn More

Learn more about the World Cup at www.fifa.com

Learn more about men's soccer at www.mlssoccer.com

Learn more about women's soccer at www.womensprosoccer.com